CULTURAL HUMILITY

DAVID A. HURLEY, SARAH R. KOSTELECKY, AND LORI TOWNSEND

ALA Editions
CHICAGO 2022

ALA Editions purchases fund advocacy, awareness, and accreditation programs for library professionals worldwide.

© 2022 by David A. Hurley, Sarah R. Kostelecky, and Lori Townsend

ISBNs
978-0-8389-4988-7 (paper)
978-0-8389-4983-2 (PDF)
978-0-8389-4981-8 (ePub)

Library of Congress Cataloging-in-Publication Data

Names: Hurley, David A., author. | Kostelecky, Sarah R., author. | Townsend, Lori, author.
Title: Cultural humility / David A. Hurley, Sarah R. Kostelecky, and Lori Townsend.
Description: Chicago : ALA Editions, 2022. | Series: ALA Editions special reports | Includes bibliographical references and index. | Summary: "This accessible and compelling Special Report introduces cultural humility, a lifelong practice that can guide library workers in their day-to-day interactions by helping them recognize and address structural inequities in library services"—Provided by publisher.
Identifiers: LCCN 2022018688 (print) | LCCN 2022018689 (ebook) | ISBN 9780838949887 (paperback) | ISBN 9780838949832 (pdf) | ISBN 9780838949818 (epub)
Subjects: LCSH: Libraries and minorities—United States. | Race awareness—United States.
Classification: LCC Z711.8 .H87 2022 (print) | LCC Z711.8 (ebook) | DDC 027.6/3—dc23/eng/20220504
LC record available at https://lccn.loc.gov/2022018688
LC ebook record available at https://lccn.loc.gov/2022018689

Series cover design by Casey Bayer. Series text design in Palatino Linotype and Interstate by Karen Sheets de Gracia.

♾ This paper meets the requirements of ANSI/NISO Z39.48-1992 (Permanence of Paper).

Printed in the United States of America
26 25 24 23 22   5 4 3 2 1

CONTENTS

"Oh no. Please don't make me do another diversity training."

This is how we* were introduced to cultural humility.

It was the one brown person on the board of a local organization that was reckoning with a problem: in a state where people of color are the majority, the board and the organization's members were overwhelmingly white. So, diversity training. The despair—the exhaustion, really—from the one dissenting board member was palpable. "How about we do something with 'cultural humility' instead," she suggested.

To be honest, it sounded like the same thing.

But the term was compelling too. Maybe because of its implied opposite: *arrogant* often seems an apt descriptor for people who refuse to recognize the importance of the cultural factors of other persons' lived realities. At the same time, though, the term *cultural humility* is itself problematic. Shouldn't we all have pride in our cultures? Black, Indigenous, and people of color (BIPOC) in the US especially are fighting many lifetimes' worth of messages that their culture is less than, undeserving, something that holds you back. Cultural *humility*?! Thanks, but we'll pass.

Queer, deaf, non-Christian, and any other people who don't see themselves in the white upper-middle-class vision of America may feel the same way. And yet, when the three of us read Tervalon and Murray-García's 1998 article introducing the concept, it resonated: rather than seek competence in interacting with people of other cultures, be open to cultural dynamics in any interaction. Let the other person determine how relevant their culture is to the interaction and be cognizant of the power imbalances. Be aware of and work to correct the structural inequities in your organization or profession, some of which come from inaccurate cultural assumptions. Understand the power imbalances present in interactions and practice critical self-reflection. This, we thought, could work in libraries.

So, this *isn't* the same old diversity workshop idea with a slightly updated wardrobe? To be honest, sometimes *cultural humility* is used that way. As we looked at journal articles and conference proceedings and workshop materials from multiple different disciplines, we found plenty of material that could have come straight from those dreaded diversity trainings. But there are also many people using the term to mean something different, something unique and, we think, useful.

---

*Throughout this report, *we* is used to refer either to the authors or to a broader group that the authors are part of, such as the collective *we* of library workers and *we* as part of humanity. We the authors note whenever our meaning of *we* changes, either by using "we all" or a similar marker that it is a generalized we, or by explicitly saying "we the authors."

Our goal for this special report is to provide readers with an understanding of cultural humility, why it is useful as an approach in libraries of all types, its relationship to other approaches, and how to develop a practice of cultural humility. We find cultural humility to be fundamentally hopeful. Transforming our libraries into more diverse, equitable, and inclusive organizations requires sustained and intentional effort, but meaningful change is not out of reach.

We hope you find it as compelling as we do.

ACKNOWLEDGMENTS

We'd like to thank our families (past and present) for their support, patience, and feedback as we wrote this volume:

Anthony Coca
Emily Lena Jones
Diana and Steven Kostelecky
Pamela and Ray Kostelecky
Heidi and Chuck Markham
James Markham
Virgil and Myrn Townsend
Rowena and Alfonso Zunie

We'd also like to thank our many colleagues and friends who helped shape our thinking on cultural humility.

And special thanks to Rachel Chance, our editor at ALA Editions, who helped us focus our writing on what was most important.

INTRODUCTION

*I*t was my first reference shift as a new hire at the Erna Fergusson branch of the Albu-
querque/Bernalillo County public library, when a young man who recognized me came
up, shook my hand and chatted briefly with me. "I know him from my last library, up on
the Navajo Nation," I offered by way of explanation to the person training me on the desk.
    "Oh," they replied. "We don't get many Navajos in here."
    I looked around the library. From the reference desk, it seemed that about a third of the
patrons were probably Navajo, including an elder wearing the distinctive traditional dress
and jewelry of Navajo women.
    How could we serve this population well, I thought, when we don't even see them?
Who was I not seeing? —David

While libraries strive to be valuable, wonderful places to the people they serve and the
people they employ, they aren't immune to being discriminatory. A recent study found
that, in online services, library employees are less likely to respond to information
requests from "Black-sounding" names, and when they do respond, their tone is less
friendly (Giulietti, Tonin, and Vlassopoulos, 2019). Problems exist behind the desk too.
Jaena Alabi (2015) found that thirty-five of the forty-one minoritized participants in her
study of academic librarians had experienced certain microaggressions, even while very
few white participants reported ever hearing them.

In some ways, it makes sense that white people do not notice microaggressions as
much as their BIPOC colleagues: microaggressions are, by definition, "indirect, subtle,
or unintentional" (Oxford University Press, 2019a). White people might really not
notice, or not see as problematic, comments or actions that people of color experience
as part of an unrelenting pattern of oppression. Needless to say, this is concerning in a
profession that remains overwhelmingly white—over 83% in 2021, according to the US
Bureau of Labor Statistics—but aspires to serve the full diversity of the population.

Diversity, equity, and inclusion in libraries is far more complex than white/non-
white, of course, but the example of unseen microaggressions illustrates a fundamental
problem: because the staff of a library is often less diverse than the community it serves,
library employees need to be aware that they are unaware of much of what people in
those communities are experiencing. Each of us needs to understand that our perspective is limited, and work to remain open to other perspectives.

Cultural humility is an approach to this work that involves an awareness of and a commitment to redressing power imbalances, a practice of honest and nondefensive self-reflection, and an orientation toward the other person that accepts and appreciates their perspective on how important their culture and identities are in any given context and interaction.

Much of the way we the authors think about cultural humility involves the idea that there is not one single objectively correct perspective. And yet, publications like this one are typically written in a third-person voice that implies and asserts a universal perspective. To resist that, we want to be open and up front with the perspectives the three of us bring to cultural humility, and why it resonates with us as individuals. Why do we feel strongly enough to write this special report to ask you, the reader, to engage with cultural humility?

Sarah: I appreciate the cultural humility concept because it acknowledges the complexity of an individual's identities that are part of our interactions with others, which connects to my lived experience as a mixed Native woman. Explaining my background, where I grew up, the origin of my family name and other personal information is part of many of my interactions with others because I do not "fit into" clearly delineated identities. Because of my experience, I am cognizant that this can often be the case for people I interact with in work and life and I try not to make assumptions about them as others make about me.

Having worked in libraries for seventeen years, I have experienced discrimination based on multiple facets of my identity, from colleagues as well as patrons, and I acknowledge the racism that exists within library practices, structures, and organizations. I have also seen the powerful impact of information in people's lives. For example, recently, someone contacted me about information on the library's Missing and Murdered Indigenous Women and Girls LibGuide (Aguilar, Kostelecky, Townsend, and Montanez, 2022), a resource I cocreated with some of my BIPOC women colleagues. The guide is curated news, reports, legislation, and organizations focused on the crisis affecting Native communities. The person shared that their family member had been murdered and they were looking for statistics to add to signs for their march for justice for the family member.

I continue to work in libraries to do my best to support others with their information needs. I believe libraries and individuals can change and do better for ourselves and our communities. I believe a cultural humility approach can support such change.

David: I spent most of my childhood in an overwhelmingly white New England suburb. Being white was completely invisible to me, much like that I was speaking English—that is to say, it was something I noticed only in people who weren't. I think because I was so comfortable in and confident of my perspective, the times I was confronted by the limitations of my worldview made a strong impact on me.

In the library, I cultivate this in my user experience (UX) work: in UX observations, I don't want to see if someone can "figure out" how to use a system, I want to see the different ways people can understand and try to solve a problem, and make sure the system works for those approaches. Good UX starts from the assumption that there is not one single "right way," and I am often reminded that the so-called commonsense way to do something is a very individual judgment.

I think this is why cultural humility appeals to me: it lets the other person show you (though not necessarily explicitly) their perspective. This feels like a holistic way toward inclusion, making space for multiple worldviews, rather than making accommodations in the one dominant worldview.

Lori: When David first introduced me to "cultural humility," I immediately thought of specific people in my professional life who made things better. They didn't make things better by knowing about my culture or using the right terms to talk about Native issues—I couldn't fairly expect a work colleague to know anything about my urban-ndn, SoCal-born, light-skinned-but-only-sorta-mixed (both my parents are from the same tribes), living-on-the-margins-of-many-cultures self. They made things better by listening and paying attention, whether to me as an individual or to the dynamics and issues present in our workplace. They found ways to do the right thing, even under pressure to maintain the status quo.

Over the course of my career in libraries, from student worker to faculty academic librarian, I have experienced plenty of microaggressions and bumped up against some structural and personal racism. But I have also experienced culturally humble colleagues, self-aware and full of humor about themselves and our sometimes absurd profession, people who have given me their time and help, and who have helped me grow and survive as a librarian; people who make the profession better. For me, cultural humility is about all of us trying to help each other. It's not about being "nice" or "perfect." It's about being kind and accurate, and making change—together, with our imperfect selves.

All three of us approach cultural humility with cautious optimism. We know that it is not a panacea for all of society's, or librarianship's, or even our own problems. We also recognize and acknowledge that cultural humility isn't the one and only answer to the enormity of the issues within librarianship around racism, diversity, equity, inclusion, and access, among others. Yet we continually find cultural humility to be a useful and potentially transformative way of being, a way to lessen harm among individuals in libraries. Its aspects of compassion and appreciation lead us to see the approach as hopeful: to hope individuals recognize that each of us has biases and beliefs that are a barrier to engaging fully with others, to hope that each of us wants to improve those interactions for the sake of each person's well-being. And to hope that each of us can expand our world to make a little more room for multiple perspectives.

2

INTRODUCING CULTURAL HUMILITY

Cultural humility was proposed by Melanie Tervalon and Jann Murray-García (1998), both medical doctors and educators, as an alternative to, and critique of, cultural competence and "the pitfall of narrowly defining competence . . . in its traditional sense: an easily demonstrable mastery of a finite body of knowledge, an endpoint evidenced largely by comparative quantitative assessments." The concern is not merely theoretical—in one of their examples, a nurse doesn't take a patient's pain seriously enough because of a cultural characteristic learned in a training. Instead, Tervalon and Murray-García envisioned a "commitment and active engagement in a lifelong process that individuals enter into on an ongoing basis with patients, communities, colleagues, and with themselves" (p. 118).

Ongoing. Process. Lifelong. These words highlight that cultural humility is something you do, a practice, rather than something you are or something you know. That isn't to say that cultural humility doesn't involve gaining knowledge. It does. But it is not a linear process of mastering content to become humble. Instead, a practice of cultural humility both requires and develops a specific understanding of the world.

We can group this understanding into two broad but connected categories. The first is personal: Understanding that one's own norms aren't actually normal. Thinking one's own values, expectations and experiences are inherently normal or universal leads to misunderstanding other people's motivations, the trade-offs they are making, and the barriers they face. This is what cultural competence programs are trying to address by teaching about cultural differences. However, rather than learning that specific groups are different in specific ways, cultural humility asks us to recognize that the person in front of us is different from us in ways we don't know and that can't be articulated. While *differences* often means differences based on race, religion, or national origin, it can be just as important between people who check those same demographic boxes. Cultural humility, hopefully, helps us see beyond those boxes.

The second category is structural: our services, policies, and literal structures can themselves be inequitable. This is the focus of critical race theory: the structural nature of inequity. An infamous example of a design that was intentionally inequitable is New York's Southern State Parkway. Robert Moses, the parkway's overtly racist designer, specified bridges to be built with low clearances so as to make it more difficult for buses, and their poorer and mostly Black passengers, to reach public beaches. While laws enshrining segregation can be overturned, rebuilding the highway system is prohibitively expensive. Even if not a single person in New York wants to restrict access to public beaches today, the structures continue to literally block mass transit.

Not all structural issues are intentional, and fortunately, not all are as difficult to dismantle. But they can also be more difficult to see, especially for people who aren't personally impacted by them. This is where these two aspects of cultural humility connect: when people think their situation is normal, they create structures that work well for them and people like them, and don't see how they will impact people less like them. Take the policy some libraries have of requiring utility bills or similarly official documents to confirm an address. Living with roommates or one's parents is just one obvious scenario where an adult might have neither.

In a very real sense, to the people affected, it doesn't matter whether structural inequities are intentional or merely thoughtless or misguided. But, for those of us designing policies and services, we can work harder to avoid and correct these issues. And this is the core of cultural humility: if we can see beyond our own experience of the world, we will be less likely to create structural inequities, more likely to recognize those that already exist, and less defensive when ones we didn't notice are pointed out to us.

What Is Normal?

Many years ago, before rideshare apps or smartphones, a colleague and I boarded an airport shuttle at Chicago's Midway airport heading to a conference hotel across town. I was the only white person in the shuttle—an unusual experience for me in conference cities. While no one knew each other, there was a lot of friendly chatting and laughter among the passengers and driver. As someone who usually rides in silence, it was tiring for me, even though I didn't really participate in the conversations. My colleague did, though, and the other passengers soon realized we were on the wrong shuttle, heading in the wrong direction! After a brief detour, we were transferred to a different shuttle. The difference was striking. Aside from the driver, my colleague was the only nonwhite person in the van. Apart from us, the passengers all wore business suits. A few had something to read, but mostly we just stared straight ahead, not exchanging a single word. Honestly, I am much more comfortable riding in silence. Had we boarded the correct shuttle to begin with, the silent men in suits would have seemed perfectly ordinary to me. I wouldn't have noticed the silence. But now it felt to me like socially awkward silence, and I could tell how uncomfortable my colleague was. As the silence wore on, I had to stifle giggles over how weird it seemed after the friendly camaraderie of the first ride. And had we boarded this shuttle first, I probably would have thought my colleague was uncomfortable because she hadn't traveled much and wasn't used to being in a big city. I would not have connected it to the odd behavior of the people around us. —David

3

CULTURAL HUMILITY IN RELATION TO OTHER APPROACHES

Cultural humility originated as part of a critique of cultural competence programs and, as discussed above, shares some insights with its predecessor. Critical race theory also influences cultural humility. Both of these frameworks are prevalent in library conversations about diversity, equity, and inclusion in libraries, and are worth a brief look here.

CULTURAL COMPETENCE

Cultural competence has been the dominant framework for looking at culture in a variety of service professions, including healthcare, social work, and education, as well as librarianship, and so is probably at least somewhat familiar to most people who are involved in library work.

An early and influential definition of cultural competence comes from Terry Cross and colleagues (1989): "Cultural competence is a set of congruent behaviors, attitudes, and policies that come together in a system, agency or among professionals and enable that system, agency or those professionals to work effectively in cross-cultural situations" (p. iv). While Cross was writing for social work, cultural competence had been a hot topic in business circles decades earlier, when American businessmen began managing their companies' new foreign offices. Just as the "tacit assumption" (Linfield, 1960, p. 41) that geography was the only change needed when working internationally gave way to "a spreading uneasy feeling that something is different about foreign operations" (Priceman, 1965, p. 5), Mark Priceman's explicit assumption that differences among Americans are eroded "by the unifying power of a common national culture" (p. 5) has given way to an understanding that there are indeed cultural differences that must be taken into account domestically as well.

There were calls for librarians to develop cultural competence starting in the early 1990s, but efforts flourished in the 2010s. In an influential article, Montiel Overall (2009) advocated for the use of the cultural competence framework by libraries and identified specific actions librarians could take to demonstrate competence. A few years later, the Association of College and Research Libraries (ACRL) published cultural competence standards for academic libraries with specific outcomes for individual employees, library administrators and the organization as a whole (ACRL Racial and Ethnic Diversity Committee, 2012). And for years, sessions on cultural competence have been ubiquitous in local and national library conferences, staff training days, and other professional development opportunities.

Many of the people who are engaged in this work recognize the pitfalls and limitations that Tervalon and Murray-García highlighted in 1998. In recent years, proponents have focused more on structural inequities and are explicit about cultural competence being a lifelong learning process, rather than the quick fix of learning the "right way" to interact with people from specific backgrounds. The way people talk about cultural competence today incorporates many of the ideas that we admire in cultural humility. Some suggest that cultural humility is a part, or an extension, of cultural competence. But the word *competence* is part of the language of qualifications and assessments that organizations use in professional development. Using this language can imply that diversity, equity, and inclusion (DEI) is primarily a hiring and training project—a framing that is familiar and comfortable to organizations. And that is the path where the pitfalls lay, where libraries can slip into thinking that progress on DEI largely requires the straightforward mastery of knowledge that employees "should know and, where appropriate, be able to employ" (American Library Association, 2009, p. 1).

We think there is value in remembering cultural humility's origin as a response to these pitfalls in cultural competence, and recognizing it as a distinct approach to issues of diversity, equity, and inclusion.

What's in a Handshake?

When, as a young white American, I moved from the East Coast to the Navajo Nation, there were cultural differences that put me off balance. One thing that felt familiar though—even comfortable—were the frequent handshakes. Handshakes had been common when I spent time with my grandparents. It seemed I was always greeting distant relatives with a firm grip and a brief-but-vigorous shake. So, when people extended their hands to me on the Navajo Nation, I didn't give it a thought. I grabbed, squeezed, and shook. But as often as not, the hand I was shaking seemed to lie limp as I crushed it in my own. I felt bad about potentially hurting the other person's hand, but the stronger reaction was to the handshake itself. Honestly, it was almost repulsive to me. I don't know that I was ever explicitly taught negative associations with soft handshakes, though a quick web search as I'm writing this found that there are many.

Somewhere along the way, someone must have explained to me that Diné people don't shake hands so much as hold them. Suddenly it made sense. Once I understood this, the gesture seemed much more intimate to me than what I had been doing. That took a little getting used to, but finally I felt I was in the know—I could competently shake hands in the Diné way!

Unfortunately for my hands, I wasn't the first white person anyone had ever met. Now, as often as not, my hands were getting crushed by people who knew that a white man would appreciate a firm handshake. For me, the handshake became a ritual of trying to guess what the other person would do, as they probably were guessing what I would do. Getting a soft handshake suddenly felt like a compliment. Context was important too. Workplace handshakes could go either way, but handshakes at ceremonies or other community events were almost always Diné style. In a forthcoming publication, Rhiannon Sorrell, a librarian at Diné College, writes about how handshakes can be fraught even for her as a Diné person navigating professional, community, and generational identities. —*David*

CRITICAL RACE THEORY

When we started working on this report, we thought critical race theory would be something that most librarians—especially those outside academic or law libraries—had given little thought to, if they had heard of it at all. As we finish, it is in the headlines almost daily, with legislation proposed in several states to outlaw teaching it. In this context, providing an overview of critical race theory is too complex and too important for the space available here. Instead, we encourage you to read a more in-depth introduction, such as Richard Delgado and Jean Stefancic's *Critical Race Theory: An Introduction* (2001). For our purposes, we will just highlight a few important ideas.

The first is intersectionality. Imagine you are a Black woman trying to get a job at a company that refuses to hire Black women. In the US, there are laws that make it illegal to discriminate on the basis of race or sex, so you should be able to sue the company to force them to make amends. You might even think your case would be especially strong, as you are being discriminated against based on two protected classes. But the company hires Black people, though they are all men, and the company hires women, though they are all white. From a legal perspective, the employer is not practicing either race- or sex-based discrimination. It is only Black women who are being refused employment. Suddenly what seemed a clearcut discrimination case is difficult to prove. Our hypothetical is based on a real case used by Kimberlé Crenshaw (1989), one of the early critical race theorists, to develop intersectionality as a legal concept in the 1980s. Tellingly, Crenshaw notes, white men suing for discrimination are not subject to the same judicial reasoning: that Black men and white women are not being discriminated against in an organization does not pose a problem in proving discrimination against white men. "Black women are perceived as a compound class because they are two steps removed from a white male norm, while white males are apparently not perceived to be a compound class because they somehow represent the norm" (p. 143).

In recent years, the concept of intersectionality has spread from law to the social sciences, education, and even the general public, as a model for understanding how multiple facets of one's identity can interplay, including in unique forms of discrimination or oppression.

The second key idea from critical race theory is that of structural racism. In the legal arena in which critical race theory developed, this is the idea that racism isn't a problem that impacts the legal system (e.g., through racist judges and juries, and specific racist laws) but rather a problem of the justice system itself. What is essential here is what this means for attempts to combat inequities in the justice system. If the legal framework is fundamentally fair, or "neutral," then our focus needs to be eliminating day-to-day racism. In this case, approaches aimed at helping individuals overcome racist beliefs are best for solving racial disparities in the United States. However, if our systems reinforce a white-dominant power structure even when working correctly, eliminating racist beliefs will not have much immediate impact on the fairness with which minoritized groups are treated.

How can a law or policy be racist if the people implementing it are not themselves racist? One possibility is that it stems from a faulty assumption that everyone is "like us" as the policy is created. Though there is a long history of intentionally discriminatory voting laws, let's imagine a well-intentioned group of people trying to create voting policy from scratch. They all drove to the meeting, so it seems requiring a state-issued photo ID to vote is common sense, as "everyone" has a driver's license. Of course, if you live in an urban area and use public transit, you don't drive and have no need for a license. But anyone can get an ID, right? Even if the answer were yes, if people without licenses are disproportionately from minoritized communities, this is a barrier to voting that does not exist for the population at large. Anyone who has spent time in their Department of Motor Vehicles will attest that this isn't a trivial matter. And, if you need to miss work to do so, the financial impacts are also not trivial.

For some people, the burden is greater. Many people—especially elders born at home in Native communities—may not have the documentation needed to get a state ID, making the process more arduous. While the number of individuals in this situation is tiny compared to the overall US population, it disproportionately impacts the ability to vote for members of one race, making it an issue of structural racism even without any racist intent.

The assumption of pure intent in this example is, of course, naive at best. A long history of actively disenfranchising Black, Native, and other people of color makes ill intentions the more plausible explanation than innocent ignorance among political operatives. Indeed, most examples of structural racism do have their roots in explicitly racist policies or assumptions, the effects of which can long outlast the specific policies themselves.

While critical race theory is useful in understanding the structural roots of many current problems, it doesn't necessarily provide guidance in navigating the day-to-day interactions within these structures. Knowing the structural inequalities of the Southern State Parkway doesn't help the drivers on the way to the beach. Cultural humility pairs an openness to the insights that critical race theory can provide, with an approach to interpersonal interactions that works to reduce harm in the moment.

4

DEFINING
CULTURAL HUMILITY

Tervalon and Murray-García did not explicitly define cultural humility when they introduced the concept, but since then, many definitions have been proposed, emphasizing different aspects for specific contexts. Here is how we define it for librarianship:

> Cultural humility involves the ability to maintain an interpersonal stance that is other oriented in relation to aspects of cultural identity that are most important to the other person, the ability to recognize the context in which interactions occur, and a commitment to redress power imbalances and other structural issues to benefit all parties (Hurley, Kostelecky, and Townsend 2019).

What does it mean to be other oriented in relation to aspects of cultural identity? On the simplest level, this means avoiding stereotyping or prejudging people. But this version of treating people as individuals is not at all the same as so-called colorblindness—the idea of not noticing someone's race or other cultural or identity markers. It isn't that those differences don't matter, but rather that one does not actually know someone else's identity, or how that identity has impacted them, or how they see that identity impacting this particular interaction. Ultimately, it is an acceptance that every interaction is affected by culture, but in ways one can't necessarily predict, understand, or maybe even see. For people in a position of relative power in the interaction—for example, by being an employee of the library where the other person is a patron—it is also maintaining an openness to the possibility that the inherent and perhaps appropriate power differential in that situation is impacting the other person in problematic ways that may not be obvious from a position of power.

What does it mean to recognize the context in which an interaction occurs? The role of culture is different (though not necessarily less) in a staff meeting than in, say, a community celebration. It is also different in an interaction between a doctor and a patient, or a librarian and a patron. The role of culture changes by context, by person, and by a host of other intangible factors. There is also historical context, as well as personal, organizational, local, national, and other contexts that come into play.

No one can know all the relevant history going into an interaction. But maintaining an awareness that there can be history, known and unknown, impacting the interaction—just as there can be power imbalances, recognized and unrecognized—is an important part of practicing cultural humility.

What does it mean to redress power imbalances and other structural issues to benefit all parties? Power differentials are not inherently bad; a library employee necessarily has more power over, say, circulation transactions than a patron does. But even without ill intent, these differentials can negatively impact services. In our discussion of critical race theory, we explored the importance of recognizing structural inequities. Cultural humility asks us not only to acknowledge them, but to commit to redressing them. A collection development librarian might have to seek out materials that are not available through the usual vendors, and that disrupt the usual ordering workflow, in order to bring different voices into the collection.

Even when the intention is there, however, redressing problems can be unexpectedly difficult. Take, for example, a policy that gives library staff the discretion to waive fines and fees below some dollar amount if it poses a financial hardship on a patron. This seems like a reasonable accommodation that balances the needs of the library with the situation of the patron. However, this policy looks very different from the different perspectives involved. While some library workers may prefer more clear-cut policies, many will be happy to be able to waive fines, and feel good about helping their patrons. For the patron, though, needing to ask for financial assistance can be difficult or embarrassing, enough so that some will instead choose to avoid the library altogether.

While this type of policy is intended to mitigate the barrier that fines create, it also reinforces the power differentials between staff and patron. And these power differentials can manifest in highly problematic ways, based on the values, biases, or prejudices of the person with power. Many years ago, when a patron at a local library complained about the five-dollar fee to replace a lost library card, the employee's response was, "How much was that tattoo on your arm?" A different employee mentioned that she routinely waived that fee for everyone, whether they asked or not, "unless they are homeless."

If a library charges fines, it is certainly better to have a way to waive them than not. But thinking it through from multiple perspectives can prevent creating policies that unnecessarily exacerbate power dynamics and lead to problematic enforcement. And if the goal of the fines is to prevent overdue materials, for example, perhaps there is a better way than fines to achieve that end.

Working to Change Power Imbalances

In 2016, Indigenous people around the world were coming together to protest against the building of the Dakota Access Pipeline. Many went in person to support the #NoDAPL movement, while others engaged locally, contributing funds, food, clothing, time, and prayers. I supported the effort in these ways but also thought I might use my voice as a librarian to raise the visibility of the issue by sharing Indigenous perspectives about what was happening. This led to me developing a LibGuide about the issue that gathered information in a variety of formats and from different sources, selecting resources that centered Native people through quotes, first-person narratives, and media (Kostelecky, 2022). I hoped the guide would be useful for people to find Indigenous perspectives about why this movement was historic and important. The LibGuide was my way to advocate for Indigenous people and our voices in library digital collections, and a way to push back against mainstream narratives, which often misrepresented the movement. —*Sarah*

5

CULTURE AND HUMILITY

Culture is "what people do" (Deitering, 2015). We start with this, the briefest possible definition, because it highlights the ubiquity of culture and is as inclusive as possible as to what constitutes culture. If culture is what people do, everything someone does has a cultural aspect.

Culture is "what people think, what people do, and what people make" and "is shared, learned, transmitted cross-generationally, symbolic, adaptive, and integrated" (Tharp, 2005, p. 3). This definition highlights that culture arises from groups, but that it changes and is "constantly contested" (Tascón & Gatwiri, 2020, p. 2) by the members of these groups. Most relevant to cultural humility is the understanding that culture is not a monolith. Individuals will express their culture individually. Culture is a moving target, not something that can be pinpointed or mastered.

And, as a final definition, "culture is what gives meaning to our lives" (Tascón and Gatwiri, 2020, p. 2). Human beings are social animals who make meaning together. Culture is our expression of that meaning. While it is a slippery concept, culture is undeniably important—and largely unknowable to outsiders.

While culture is difficult to define, humility can be a difficult concept to understand. It often engenders strong reactions, both positive and negative: being humble may be an admirable quality, but few hope their children will come from humble beginnings. It is a trait often associated with religion or the religious—think of the ritual of the pope washing the feet of juvenile delinquents or migrants—and in an increasingly secular US society, that connotation might prove a barrier to some. Humbling oneself typically is associated with submitting oneself to authority, or bowing down before someone or something outside ourselves—imagery that, at the very least, brings up troubling power dynamics.

Psychologists—in particular those working in the subfield of positive psychology— understand humility a bit differently. Humility, as defined by the researcher June Price Tangney (2000), means admitting we as individuals aren't perfect. She argues that there are several dimensions of humility, which she calls a "neglected virtue":

- [an] accurate assessment of one's abilities and achievements (not low self-esteem, self-deprecation).
- [an] ability to acknowledge one's mistakes, imperfections, gaps in knowledge, and limitations (often vis-à-vis a "higher power").
- openness to new ideas, contradictory information, and advice.

- keeping one's abilities and accomplishments—one's place in the world—in perspective (e.g., seeing oneself as just one person in the larger scheme of things).
- [a] relatively low self-focus, a "forgetting of the self," while recognizing that one is but part of the larger universe. [And]
- [an] appreciation of the value of all things, as well as the many different ways that people and things can contribute to our world. (pp. 73–74)

The most initially surprising element of humility for us the authors was the concept of "an accurate assessment." The word *accurate* is a direct challenge to common definitions of humility that emphasize deprecation or underestimation. On the other hand, it has been shown that we humans often *overestimate* our positive qualities and abilities while sidelining the merits of others (Moore and Schatz, 2017). Perhaps humility's emphasis on accurate self-knowledge is not so surprising.

However, self-awareness and accurate self-assessment are notoriously challenging to achieve. Yet achievement may not be as important as the attempt:

> Our perspective on humility implies a *willingness* to see the self accurately rather than the absolute attainment of accuracy. Nonetheless, from our perspective, accuracy is secondary to whether a person is willing and able to weigh information in a nondefensive way. (Peterson and Seligman, 2004, p. 463, emphasis added)

This interpretation of accuracy repositions humility as a process rather than a goal, encouraging an attitude and a habit of mind rather than a preoccupation with how a person sees themselves. This shift leads to the most important aspect of humility: "a relatively low self-focus, a 'forgetting of the self,' while recognizing that one is but part of the larger universe" (Tangney, 2000, p. 74). This phenomenon can be referred to as becoming "unselved" (Templeton, 1997). Humility is embodied by the act of turning our gaze outward, to the other: "Our eyes are opened to the beauty and potential in those around us" (Tangney, 2000, p. 73).

Thus, the two essential features of humility can be summarized as accuracy, rather than modesty or devaluing, and becoming unselved in an appreciative and self-reflective way:

> True humility is more like self-forgetfulness. . . . It leaves people free to esteem their special talents and, with the same honesty, to esteem their neighbor's. Both the neighbor's talents and one's own are recognized as gifts and, like one's height, are not fit subjects for either inordinate pride or self-deprecation (Buri, 1988, p. 38).

When these two terms come together in the phrase *cultural humility*, it illustrates a fundamental principle: that it is impossible to really know either a person's culture or the full context of your interaction with them. There is no secret trick to making the "right" choices, acting the "right" way, and saying the "right" things. What cultural humility offers is a way to sit with your unknowing, to acknowledge the limits of your knowledge, and still move forward to build and maintain the relationships needed to make change.

CULTURAL HUMILITY AS A THRESHOLD PRACTICE

Threshold concepts are the intellectual equivalent of riding a bicycle. Once you know how, it is hard to remember struggling with it. But while you are struggling, it seems impossibly difficult to learn. More formally, within education, threshold concepts are the core ideas in a discipline that, while difficult for students to grasp, are the most meaningful ideas in a curriculum. When a student grasps these ideas—when they cross that threshold—their understanding is transformed (Meyer and Land, 2005).

Cultural humility likely involves several threshold concepts. The recognition that one's norms aren't inherently normal, or that one's own perspective isn't the only valid one, can seem obvious to the point of being facile to people who have that recognition. But it can seem counterintuitive, if not nonsensical, to those who haven't. This idea of troublesome knowledge is a hallmark of threshold concepts.

Cultural humility is troublesome in other ways too. The phrase itself, consisting of humility and culture (two concepts that are each troublesome in their own way) is troublesome language. The "other-orientation" of cultural humility can be troublesome, wrapped up in notions of who is "other," as can related concepts such as intersectionality and structural racism.

Cultural humility is transformative, both intellectually and emotionally. This, too, is a hallmark of threshold concepts. The move away from ideas of mastery can feel like an unburdening. Likewise, the shift away from knowledge acquisition to something that sounds more like a way of being or a habit of mind signals a new paradigm. And the ability to decenter one's own perspective and recognize one's norms as only one set of norms literally transforms one's view of the world and one's relation to it.

Cultural humility is also reconstitutive—another hallmark of threshold concepts. Developing an understanding of cultural humility is in no way a straight or even linear path. New understandings replace older ones, mental models need to be reconsidered and reconstructed, understanding oscillates back and forth between newer and older insights in order to make sense of how they fit together.

But cultural humility is not just a concept, even a troubling, transformative, and reconstitutive one. It is defined not only by understanding, but how a person acts based on those understandings. There is no cultural humility without individual action. It is better understood, therefore, not as a threshold concept, but as a threshold practice (Gourlay, 2009), one that strengthens and reinforces itself. The best way to learn cultural humility—the best way across that threshold—is to practice cultural humility.

PRACTICING CULTURAL HUMILITY

Practicing cultural humility is not easy. It asks all of us to accept perspectives that conflict with our own, to set aside defensiveness, to engage in critical self-reflection, and to recognize and use whatever power we have as individuals to overcome structural inequities and redress power imbalances. Each of these are abilities that are strengthened through the practice of cultural humility, meaning that the best way to develop cultural humility is to practice cultural humility.

That may not sound very helpful, so let's start with a scenario. The general issue is one we have heard of happening in a library, but the specifics and the people are made up:

Brianna is behind the circulation desk when one of the library's regulars comes in. "Hey, are my books here yet?" the young woman asks cheerfully.

"Hmm, let me check." A few weeks ago, the teenage patron had been frustrated that neither of the books she was looking for had been on the shelf, even though the catalog said they were available. Brianna had marked them missing and placed a hold, a process that would initiate a search and, if they weren't found, get replacement copies ordered.

"Huh, that's weird," Brianna says, looking at the screen. "It looks like they haven't been ordered yet." On the other side of the desk, the patron lets out a loud sigh.

"Let me call our Acquisitio—the people who do the ordering, and find out what's up," Brianna says, grabbing the phone. "Hey Erica, this is Brianna at Circ. Can you check on a couple reorder requests?" Brianna gives her colleague the relevant information, and feels her stomach drop when she gets the response:

"Oh, those are Urban Fiction titles. We don't replace those because they get stolen constantly," Erica says.

"That is some racist BS!" the patron exclaims when Brianna explains the situation.

"No, I . . ." Brianna starts, but catches herself. She takes a breath. "Sorry, I didn't mean to talk over you."

"Whatever you say," the patron says, visibly angry, and walks out of the library.

Brianna takes a few breaths, and then explains what just happened to her manager. "The policy does sound kind of racist," Brianna admits at the end.

"Yes," her manager agrees. "Erica shouldn't have said they were stolen. 'Missing' is more appropriate."

"But it's not just that. Why don't we replace Urban Fiction? It's one of our most popular collections, and we replace everything else?"

"Well, like Erica said, these get stol— . . . go missing a lot."

"Our test-prep books get stolen all. the. time. And we constantly get replacements."

"Come on. Test-prep books are different, Brianna."

Brianna just stands there, feeling her fists clench at her side.

"If you want to take it up with Acq., be my guest," her manager says. "I doubt you'll get anywhere."

Brianna slept on it that night, but not much. She was angry. The library had seemed to be making a real effort to reach out to broader communities than it had been even a few years ago. There had been some very poignant social media posts. And now one of her regulars had stormed out of the library, calling it racist. It felt like all the good work was coming undone. Or had never been real.

"Erica, can I talk to you about the Urban Fiction issue that came up yesterday?" Brianna asks the next day.

"Of course. Your manager mentioned the patron who was upset. I'm sorry about that, but I'm not going to change the policy. With that collection, it seems like every title we order gets stolen, sometimes before it even gets its first circ."

"But it's a very popular collection with our older teens and twentysomethings," Brianna argues. "Besides, we always reorder the test-prep books, and they go missing at least as often."

"The test-prep books come from a different budget line," Erica says, waving the point away.

"Well, maybe there should be a budget line for replacing Urban Fiction too." Brianna is getting angry, and it shows in her voice.

Erica sits back in her chair, crossing her arms. "Just where would you like that budget to come from? Hmm? What do you propose we stop ordering so that more copies of those books can get stolen? How are you going to explain that decision to patrons who complain that we don't have the books they like?"

Brianna takes a deep breath. "I'm just saying that my patron had a point. This sounds like a racist policy."

Erica nearly jumps out of her chair. "Did you just call me racist?! That sort of name-calling has no place in this organization. If you can't keep things civil . . . we're done here. I'll be speaking with your manager."

PEOPLE, CONTEXT, AND SITUATIONS

Let's break down this scenario by looking more closely at three elements: the people, the context, and the situation.

First, there are the participants involved in the interaction. Each person brings their own personal culture to the situation—their various identities, including their personal histories as individuals. In this scenario, Brianna is in a position of relatively less power than her manager or Erica from Acquisitions. The patron is likely BIPOC, but we the authors choose not to specify anyone else's race. Of course, a person's race or ethnicity matters a great deal. How does our understanding change, if the participants change?

Second, there's the context, which is the broad background for the interaction: the place and its geography. This can mean a geographic location but also includes other kinds of geographies, such as cultural (e.g., nation, ethnicity, race, religion) and functional (e.g., school, library, hospital). In addition to the current context, historical contexts might be important as well. If our patron is a person of color in the United States in 2022, it is quite likely that she has living family members who remember having been legally denied services at that library based on their race or skin color.

But it would be a mistake to confuse the context with the individuals living within it. Each individual is a unique being, not a culture or a gender or a race or a profession, though those things may contribute to how they see and act in the world. Knowledge about a culture does not equate to knowledge about the individuals in that culture.

Finally, there's the situation. This is the exact circumstance that brings about an interaction; the question at the circ desk, the committee meeting, the performance review, the chat over coffee. In this instance, there is the individual who wants to use the library, who reacts to a policy that will prevent her from getting the books she wants, an individual who sees the negative effects of the policy and wants it reconsidered, and a couple of individuals defending the status quo policy because of budgetary considerations.

We aren't arguing for any particular policy decision in this scenario. We want to identify what went well and what did not go well from a cultural humility perspective. We can start with Brianna. Brianna is able to stop herself from getting defensive when the patron accuses the library of racism. She works to understand the patron's perspective, and, courageously, tries to represent this perspective—and the harm the policy is causing—to the people in the organization with the power to make changes, despite encountering resistance.

But what about Brianna's manager and Erica in Acquisitions?

The manager might consider themself an ally. After all, they noticed that suggesting that a collection used primarily by young BIPOC patrons gets "stolen" is problematic, but this is a superficial understanding of the situation that leads the manager to think everything can be solved by more careful language. They can't see beyond the library's perspective of how things are valued and how decisions are made. When they see how strongly Brianna feels, they get out of her way. That's admittedly better than blocking her from bringing her concerns forward. But even if they didn't fully understand Brianna's perspective, they could have used their position of greater power in the organization to support Brianna, rather than sending her on her own to meet with Erica.

Erica, on the other hand, probably sees herself as a realist, using data to make the hard decisions about budget. She is so entrenched in the structures of the library, though, that she forgets those structures are themselves value statements. When the budget structures are challenged, she becomes defensive. Notice, too, that she hears the idea of racism only as a personal attack—an unprofessional insult—rather than as something that could conceivably be impacting how the library's budget values different genres and the patrons who use them.

It's also worth highlighting that even though Brianna was practicing cultural humility, there wasn't a positive resolution in the interaction with the patron. Over time, practicing cultural humility can help produce relationships where there is enough trust that the patron would know that Brianna will listen and take her concerns seriously. But cultural humility is not meant to be a magic bullet to make everyone happy in the moment. It is part of a long-term strategy for improving understanding, relationships, and, ultimately, services.

But what about the patron herself? Shouldn't *she* have brought a little cultural humility to her reaction to the policy? Shouldn't she have tried to understand the library's perspective? We are sharing this scenario from the perspective of the library employees, and so are focusing on what the library employees can control: their own reactions. Each person can commit to their own practice of cultural humility, but we do not want cultural humility weaponized by people in the more-powerful position as a way to criticize, silence, or discredit people in the less-powerful position. In fact, we the authors want to emphasize that this sort of analysis in which we point out various people and argue that they should be more culturally humble is only appropriate with fictional scenarios. Discussing the specifics of how actual colleagues fail at cultural humility is not what we are recommending!

We also want to be clear that we are not saying that either the patron or Brianna is correct in their assessment of the policy. More broadly, we don't mean to say that the person in the position of lower power or from the minoritized perspective is always right. The issue is how to listen and assess the opinions and insights that people are bringing from those perspectives. It would be easy to dismiss the patron's concerns: she doesn't understand how libraries make purchasing decisions. Brianna, too, could be dismissed: she doesn't know how budgets are allocated or the difficult decision-making process that goes into creating a collection that best serves the entire community. But if you value only the opinions of people for whom the structures already make sense, you can only serve to reinforce those structures.

Hearing Different Perspectives

When the COVID-19 pandemic began, I paid careful attention to our changing understanding of the disease. Like many of us, I started consulting new sources, listening to new voices, and learning new terms. However, I grew curious about the people I saw in higher education pushing for campuses to stay in-person while eschewing concerns about ventilation and even resisting precautions such as masking. In the UNM University Libraries' discussions about operating during a pandemic, I felt like a persistent gadfly, bringing up risks again and again.

When the leadership of the University Libraries proposed guidelines for returning to campus and staffing the library buildings, most seemed to think the plan was fine (at least among the people who responded to the plan publicly). Sarah and I were among the few people who voiced dissent. As we talked about this outside of the official meetings, we realized that some of the loudest and firmest critics of certain library approaches to COVID-19 were the three tenured faculty who were women of color.

Sarah and I realized that many people were evaluating conditions based on their individual risk assessment ("Yes, the risk of my getting sick under this plan is low enough that I am comfortable"); while we were mostly evaluating them based on community-risk considerations ("If we all follow this model, the risk of spread within our communities is too high for me to be comfortable with"). Understanding that there was a difference of perspective, not just a difference of opinion, would have led to decisions that addressed a broader set of concerns. But the underrepresentation of people of color in the library made it look like the chosen policies made sense to everyone except a few cranky outliers. –*Lori*

KEYS TO PRACTICING CULTURAL HUMILITY

The keys to practicing cultural humility in this scenario were:

- Don't be defensive.
- Recognize other perspectives.
- Practice critical self-reflection.

Let's look at each in more depth.

Don't Be Defensive

The first step in practicing cultural humility is to defuse your own defensiveness. That is not to say you can never defend yourself against accusations that you think are unfair. But cultural humility asks you to listen first, be willing to consider the feedback for later critical self-reflection, and separate any personal accusation from any broader point that the other person is trying to make.

The problem with an immediate defensive reaction is that it turns the discussion into one about you, and probably a heated one at that. Instead, leave the heat aside and try to access your curiosity. Assume the best intentions of the person in front of you and find out more, gently. Listen, trying to understand rather than to respond. Notice that we don't advise ignoring or discounting the racism charge in our scenario, but it isn't the focus of the best response. Setting aside the heat of accusation, it can serve to guide one's understanding of what the other person sees the issue to be. If it is an accusation that surprises you, it can serve to usefully shake up your perspective. What you want to avoid is focusing the interaction on an argument that you are not racist, or using the accusation as a way to shut down the conversation.

Not being defensive is a skill that needs practice. For many white people especially, discussions around diversity, equity, and inclusion engender feelings of defensiveness. Examine your reactions, particularly negative ones, to these ideas or discussions. To be clear, the point isn't to come to agreement with every idea. Rather, it is to understand why certain arguments trigger emotional reactions, whether or not you agree with them, and then to see whether your understanding changes when you approach an argument without defensiveness.

It is important to note that what we are discussing here is reacting to arguments that are coming from someone with a less-powerful position. While it may or may not be useful to engage this way with arguments that attempt to reinforce the status quo, doing so is not an act of cultural humility.

Recognize Other Perspectives

This, too, is a skill that needs to be cultivated. Being able to see other perspectives helps prevent incorrect assumptions from interfering in your interactions. It also helps you recognize that structures such as policies, practices, and even technologies embed certain values and embody certain perspectives that themselves can be examined. Finally, without the ability to recognize that your perspective is only one of many, real communication with people different from you will not be possible.

People who work in libraries are well positioned to find diverse perspectives: seek out stories written from perspectives other than your own, and for which you are not the primary audience. The goal is not to master knowledge about different groups, but to gain insight and understanding. Michael Mungin, the librarian who maintains an online filmography of queer and trans people of color, suggests that seeking out individual voices from a group you aren't part of is an important technique for reducing bias and discrimination (Mungin, forthcoming). But do beware of stories written by people outside of the cultural group represented in the story, as these can easily serve to reinforce a dominant perspective.

Techniques from user experience work can also be useful here, as well as user-centered design. From Erica-in-Acquisitions' perspective, the policy of not purchasing replacement copies of books in a certain genre makes budgetary sense. Had she put herself in the shoes of the patron who wanted those books, the policy—that missing books will be replaced by request except for those that appeal primarily to young BIPOC audiences—might look a bit different. This is where learning and thinking about context is important as well. If you don't understand the history and larger social context that people work and exist in, you risk reducing your understanding of the interaction to the individual and their personality.

Context is also where the power differentials and imbalances are reckoned with—power imbalances that may have built up over decades, that may be so embedded in the place that they can go unnoticed. This includes historical events that have resonated down through decades and centuries (e.g., legal and de facto segregation, genocide, redlining, entrenched poverty), but also the more individual power differentials of daily life, (e.g., full time versus part time, "professional" status versus "paraprofessional" status, supervisor versus supervised).

Learning about the history of the place, the cultures that have historically dwelled and interacted there, invites this knowledge into the interaction and helps the participants recognize the overlapping geographies at play. Approaches like critical race theory are essential to this work.

Being able to see other perspectives is a large part of having an other orientation, but it is also useful in helping to see the limits of your own point of view. This brings us to our third element: critical self-reflection.

Checking Assumptions

At Diné College, I was chatting with an instructor, also non-Navajo, who was frustrated by students who regularly fell asleep during his class. I don't remember the discussion exactly, but the implication was clear: these students are not taking college seriously. He had warned one student that he wouldn't pass the class if he didn't get to bed on time, to no effect. A short time later, I picked up a young guy hitchhiking (that being a common form of transportation on the Navajo Nation) who turned out to be a student heading to class. I don't know if he was the same student my colleague complained about, but he fell asleep almost as soon as he got in my car. When he woke up, I asked, "Long night?" "Nah," he shrugged, and matter-of-factly explained how he gets up at 4 a.m. to deal with the cattle, then hitchhikes the sixty or so miles to the nearest off-reservation city where he has a part-time job at a convenience store, and then hitchhikes back to campus, where he's a full-time student.

Falling asleep during class is problematic regardless, but the assumption of irresponsible students staying up all night got in the way of seeing someone very driven. This student needed some sort of support, not an admonishment to get more sleep. —*David*

Practice Critical Self-Reflection

Cultural humility is mostly other oriented; however, you do have to know yourself to get out of your own way. Critical self-reflection involves examining your beliefs, perspectives, identity, and culture in order to understand the context that you bring to an interaction. This is a chance to consider how aspects of your identity impact how you see the world, and how the world sees you.

In our scenario, neither Erica nor the manager react well. Had they been able to defuse their defensive responses and see other perspectives, the interactions likely would have progressed differently and resulted in more positive outcomes. But what would have helped them do that? A moment of self-reflection. That sounds simple, but a pause for self-reflection is often extremely difficult to manifest in the moment. Chances are, those who can stop in the moment have built up that skill through practice. Brianna's deep breath was something she did intentionally in response to her own reaction. The most important time for self-reflection, though, is after an interaction, in reflecting on how you might have been more kind, listened more fully, valued the person more completely.

Critical self-reflection also includes understanding your own responses. Why did you get defensive? What assumptions were you making? Which of your values were involved? Self-reflection can also include reflecting on the library or other group or organization you identify (or are identified) with.

Self-Reflection

At my student job in college, there was another student employee who was also a Native woman. I was glad to meet her and excited to work with her but as I tried different times to talk to her, to get to know her, she didn't seem anything more than cordial. I assumed her lack of conversation meant she didn't like me, so I backed off trying to connect with her. I can't pinpoint how now, but we were able to eventually build our friendship and continue to be close friends today.

I didn't tell her I thought she didn't like me at first, but one day she shared with me her frustration with people who would cut her off in conversations and assume she didn't have anything to say. She said it wasn't that she didn't want to talk or was shy, but she had to take a minute to think before she spoke because her Native language is her first language and English is her second language. She often processed things in her first language, then translated back to English. Hearing her say this made me reflect on my initial impression of her and how I had wrongly interpreted her behavior toward me. I realized I had probably initially behaved the same as those people upsetting her, talking without giving her a chance to respond and making assumptions about what I felt was a lack of engagement.

I appreciate my friend articulating her frustration to me, because I think of her when I work with colleagues or patrons who may initially seem reserved, quiet, or difficult to engage with. I try to remember that my idea of "friendly" or conversational behaviors are not universal, and to be open to engaging with someone who has different ways of expressing those behaviors. —*Sarah*

8

CULTURAL HUMILITY
AND ORGANIZATIONS

So far, we the authors have discussed cultural humility only in terms of individuals. What about an institution itself? Can a library be culturally humble? Frankly, we aren't entirely sure what that would mean. Perhaps that policies are created and services are designed by groups of individuals, and implemented and enforced by individuals, all of whom are practicing cultural humility? Even in this case, it would be up to the individual to practice cultural humility. The organizational role would be limited to creating an environment that encourages individuals to develop and strengthen a cultural humility practice.

How can libraries do this? The first instinct might be to hold workshops. Workshops have their place, but, as alluded to in our preface, can be especially burdensome for BIPOC and other minoritized employees. When people groan at well-intentioned plans for diversity workshops, reading groups on diversity, or similar group activities, it is based on negative experiences in those settings. Especially if the workshop is not led by a professional facilitator, BIPOC are often expected to "share" embarrassing and painful anecdotes to help white colleagues' understanding. In the authors' experience, people say things that are problematic, if not outright offensive, and the BIPOC folks in the room will either have to stay silent (and be accused of not wanting to have "difficult but important" conversations) or be forced to explain and sometimes argue about why those things are problematic. This can feel like we are defending our own humanity to our colleagues. It is often not a positive experience.

The profession is caught in a kind of catch-22 in thinking about diversity workshops and other such educational and consciousness-raising efforts. People want to learn and do better. We the authors want to learn and do better. However, if participants do not approach these settings with an attitude of cultural humility, these workshops risk making things worse. Workshops, then, should not be offered lightly, and not as a first step to addressing issues of diversity, equity, and inclusion in an organization.

What library leadership can do, however, is develop cultural humility in themselves. They can prioritize having multiple perspectives involved in decision-making and planning. They can prioritize bringing individuals with those diverse perspectives into the organization in a variety of ways, the most important of which is through hiring decisions. They can encourage their employees to express concerns or dissent, and make sure they understand the reasons for differences of opinion. Library leadership can lead culturally humble reviews of policies and practices—again, with people who bring multiple perspectives, to ensure that policies and practices exist for a legitimate purpose (rather than, say, "to teach personal responsibility" to public library patrons, something that is outside the scope of public library services), and that their implementation does not create or exacerbate inequities.

"They Will Never Understand Us."

Early in my career, I was sitting at the reference desk when a colleague came up and started visiting about a recent wedding she had attended. It was a wedding from another culture, and she described some of the traditions and ceremonies she found interesting, confusing, and also off putting (clothing she compared to pajamas, treatment of women). She declared, "I will never understand tribal cultures!" in an exasperated tone. She was clearly using the word *tribal* as a synonym for *alien, backward, narrow-minded,* and *parochial*. She was also unconsciously echoing something my father had said to me not long before that: "They will never understand tribal people"—meaning they will never understand us.

At the time, I remember feeling quietly nervous that she would remember I was a tribal person, and also being quietly offended. I didn't say anything, and she never knew what I thought about what she said. I'm sure any person of color reading this will have experienced similar situations (and worse), and we all know the kinds of risks we take in saying something: having to sort through and experience even more ignorant and hurtful statements, having to help someone process their feelings/thoughts about the situation, getting into a long conversation when you don't have time, yourself being accused of something because you made someone feel defensive, somehow offending them because you didn't express your concern in the "right" way, and so on. So we often don't say anything—it is usually the better option. I would say something to a colleague I trusted, typically a culturally humble colleague, who would take my saying something as a gift, not get defensive, and not turn the exchange into a giant deal about them and their feelings. —*Lori*

9

CULTURAL HUMILITY
REFLECTED IN LEADERSHIP

A practice of cultural humility is essential at all levels of the library. But the nature of hierarchical organizations is such that the attitudes and behaviors of directors, deans, and other high-level leaders have an outsize impact on organizations and organizational culture. Leaders who practice cultural humility can transform an organization. To illustrate this, we share two stories of leaders who we feel have exhibited a practice of cultural humility to positive effect.

MAYOR LANDRIEU AND THE CONFEDERATE STATUES IN NEW ORLEANS

In 2017, the city of New Orleans removed its final monument celebrating the Confederacy, a statue of Robert E. Lee. Mayor Mitch Landrieu marked this final removal with a speech in which he spoke of the history of New Orleans as a major port in the slave trade. He asked why there are "no slave ship monuments, no prominent markers on public land to remember the lynchings or the slave blocks." He described this lack as a "lie by omission." He also asserted that the monuments in question "purposefully celebrate a fictional, sanitized Confederacy; ignoring the death, ignoring the enslavement, and the terror that it actually stood for." ("Mitch Landrieu's Speech on the Removal of Confederate Monuments in New Orleans," 2017).

Landrieu's exceptional speech contains several markers of cultural humility. He described listening to the stories of those negatively impacted by the monuments. In particular, he asked himself to consider how African American parents could possibly explain these monuments to their children. This deep listening and reflection without defensiveness is cultural humility in action. And though the motivations for his actions were clear to him at the moment in time he delivered his speech, he admitted that he spent many years not even noticing the monuments, and said, "So I am not judging anybody. We all take our own journey on race."

He also celebrated the contributions of New Orleans: "We radiate beauty and grace in our food, in our music, in our architecture, in our joy of life, in our celebration of death; in everything we do." This appreciative reflection is inclusive and joyful, another marker of cultural humility.

Landrieu quoted remarks President Barack Obama made at the opening of the National Museum of African American History and Culture. That museum houses an object described as a "stone with a flattened top and bottom, squared back and sides, and a rounded front used as a slave auction block in Hagerstown, Maryland. A rectangular metal plaque is screwed to the top of the stone, with embossed text reading 'GENERAL ANDREW JACKSON / AND HENRY CLAY / SPOKE FROM THIS SLAVE BLOCK / IN HAGERSTOWN / DURING THE YEAR 1830'" (National Museum of African American History and Culture, n.d.).

> Consider what this artifact tells us about history. . . . On a stone where day after day, for years, men and women were . . . bound, and bought and sold, and bid [on] like cattle; on a stone worn down by the tragedy of over a thousand bare feet—for a long time, the only thing we considered important, the singular thing we once chose to commemorate as "history" with a plaque[,] were the unmemorable speeches of two powerful men. (Office of the Press Secretary, 2016)

Both these leaders are speaking of unheard stories. Retelling and fostering these overlooked and omitted narratives encourages a shift of perspective, for sure, but can also be seen as examples of seeking accuracy in our understanding—another feature of cultural humility. In the end, what makes Mayor Landrieu an example of a culturally humble leader isn't his words or even the fact that he truly heard his constituents, but that he took substantive action to redress the wrongs revealed through that listening.

PROVOST ABDALLAH AND THE UNM SEAL

The UNM student body has consistently included a sizable number of Native American students, 9% of the student population in 2021 (University of New Mexico, n.d.). This is not surprising in a state with twenty-three recognized tribes who make up 10.5% of the state population.

Imagine you are one of these students attending your graduation ceremony. Your family is there to celebrate your accomplishment. You're excited at the possibilities your future holds as you are moments away from becoming a college graduate, maybe the first one in your family. But then you look down and notice the UNM seal on your diploma. There are two figures around the UNM letters: a conquistador with a sword and a fringe-clad, Kit Carson–like frontiersman with a gun. You look at the podium on the stage and see the image again.

You think: How did I not notice this image before? Why is my school using these violent colonial representations that ignore my people and culture at this celebration that includes me? You feel unnerved but try to remember the happiness you felt earlier and try not to look at the image for the rest of the ceremony.

This scenario could have been the experience of many UNM Native American students from 1909 until 2017, when the official seal with these figures was taken out of use. The decision was hard won, taking years of student and community protest against the image, including a recommendation from the campus Equity and Inclusion Office to stop use of the image and a group letter of support whose signatories included university library employees.

During one of many protests against the seal, then UNM President Robert Frank was witnessed arguing angrily with protestors who had entered the administrative building. However, Provost Chaouki Abdallah was seen chatting quietly with protestors outside the building; he didn't participate in the protest, but he appeared to be listening. When Frank left UNM, Abdallah stepped in as acting president and allowed a series of public forums to take place to discuss the issue of the seal with the wider UNM community. When the UNM Board of Regents wouldn't allow changes to the seal, Acting President Abdallah used the power he had to issue an official university-wide decision to stop using it. Eventually, a new seal was approved by the regents in December of 2020. While the student and community leaders deserve the bulk of the credit for this outcome, Abdallah listened to his community and allowed them to lead on this issue. The story of the UNM Seal illustrates cultural humility concepts such as centering the experience of the other person, intellectual humility, and challenging power structures.

Powerful individuals within an organization are positioned to make an impact. Often they choose to support and maintain the status quo that brought them to positions of power. However, leaders can choose to take actions that challenge existing power structures. Even reactive action is better than indifference, even when that action simply involves supporting an agenda that less-powerful individuals and groups have worked to build.

10

CRITIQUES OF CULTURAL HUMILITY

THE PROBLEM OF HUMILITY AND MINORITIZED PEOPLE

While we the authors believe in the usefulness of cultural humility, we recognize people may be skeptical of the concept and practice, especially among BIPOC. We, too, have had questions and felt uncertainty, and occasionally still do. We want to identify some of the concerns we and others have with cultural humility and share our thinking on them.

CULTURAL PRIDE AND CULTURAL HUMILITY, OR, IS THIS ONLY FOR WHITE PEOPLE (PART 1)?

Early in the process of researching and learning about cultural humility, two of the authors, Lori and Sarah, both Native women, thought, wait, do we really need to work on our humility? Is cultural humility something that only white people need? Or, worse, is it just another way to get BIPOC folks to humble ourselves? Is this about us making ourselves even smaller and less threatening so that we don't make others feel uncomfortable? What about the pride we feel, and encourage others to feel, when thinking about our culture and our identities?

We wondered, what does pride even mean? For that, we went to the dictionary. The first definition of *pride* from the Oxford English Dictionary (Oxford University Press, 2019b) is: "A high, esp. an excessively high, opinion of one's own worth or importance which gives rise to a feeling or attitude of superiority over others; inordinate self-esteem." That definition doesn't seem to accurately reflect the pride people are expressing during cultural events such as the annual Rock Your Mocs Day, during which Indigenous students wear their moccasins to classes and around campus.

Another OED definition is more useful: "A consciousness of what befits, is due to, or is worthy of oneself or one's position; self-respect; self-esteem, esp. of a legitimate or healthy kind or degree" (ibid.). This definition seems more applicable to the cultural pride BIPOC folks have and is not counter to humility—especially given humility's defining characteristic of accuracy.

Perceptions of Positionality

As part of a promotion-and-tenure process, I wrote a statement for colleagues about my scholarship and why I research specific topics. I wrote about my research being grounded in Indigenous methodologies, done to improve the lives of Indigenous people, and why these methods are important to me as a Native faculty member and Native person. Members of the promotion-and-tenure committee provide feedback on these statements before they are sent to the campus review committee. A senior, tenured colleague on the committee read my statement and described my focus on Indigenous methods and articulating my positionality as a Native woman as "risky." Though I was initially taken aback, I responded that I was going to take this chance to push my colleagues to read about these methods and force them to acknowledge me as a Native faculty member and to "see" me, even if only this one time—to which my colleague didn't respond and instead dropped the issue.

Thinking about this exchange later, I wondered if the colleague was either implying that I was trying to get some advantage by highlighting my identity, or that by reiterating the ways my being Native informs my research, colleagues would grow tired of reading about it, or both. To me, I was trying to be clear about the why and how of my scholarship, not overstating the impact of my Indigeneity but not downplaying it either. I kept the statement as it was but still wonder how many colleagues may have thought similarly as this person did about my work. —*Sarah*

Mainstream culture may have taught BIPOC folks to internalize dominant narratives that are inaccurate and harmful. Humility encourages us to seek accuracy, inasmuch as that is possible, and to appreciate those true things that we discover. We believe that BIPOC can practice cultural humility in our interactions with people while still having pride in the multiple identities that each individual embodies. Cultural humility and cultural pride are not incompatible.

CENTERING WHITENESS, OR, IS THIS ONLY FOR WHITE PEOPLE (PART 2)?

It seems that all the approaches to living and working in pluralistic communities struggle with centering whiteness. That is, it is easy for a framework to implicitly reinforce the idea that the norms of the dominant group, middle- to upper-class white people in the US, are normal, even while explicitly arguing for the diversity and subjectivity of norms. Tascón and Gatwiri (2020), for example, make a strong case for this happening in cultural competence.

But whereas the idea of cultural competence was developed by white Americans concerned with how to behave or act appropriately in foreign countries and cultures, cultural humility was envisioned by people of color seeing the limits of cultural competence within their workplaces in the US. So it might seem that cultural humility must be "better" at decentering whiteness. However, this is something that all approaches, including cultural humility and critical race theory, must actively contend with. They are all being adopted in contexts where a dominant perspective exists—and the people with that dominant perspective are the ones for whom seeing other perspectives is both the hardest challenge and, because they are often in positions of power, the most important.

And yet, if cultural humility is allowed to center whiteness, its power is erased. People who hold the dominant perspective are poorly served by an approach that reinforces it as the norm—that's the exact opposite of the goal. For everyone else, it becomes, at best, irrelevant. This would be a shame, as true and lasting change is only possible if everyone is involved in bringing that change.

In thinking and writing about cultural humility, we the authors have had to contend with this issue of centering whiteness again and again. We have sought to view cultural humility from and through different perspectives, trying to understand how the approach would work with all kinds of people in a variety of situations and contexts. And we think it does work. We think cultural humility has value for everyone, that we all benefit from decentering our own perspective. We also think that the *practice* of cultural humility explicitly decenters whiteness, even if *discussions* of cultural humility can fall into the trap of reinforcing it.

COMPLEXITY OF POWER DIFFERENTIALS

What about situations where there are multiple, conflicting forms of power?

The library employee is in a position of power over patrons. But what if the person behind the circ desk is a student employee and the patron is her professor? What if the employee is BIPOC from a working-class background, in a public library serving a very wealthy, very white community? What if a BIPOC manager is managing an all-white staff?

In each of these cases, the position does give the person power in the situation. But the power that comes with being a library assistant, or even a library director, is circumscribed. The power structures of broader society are also very much in play, and may be far more salient to everyone involved. This is a thorny issue, and one where, again, it may seem that cultural humility is a tool only for white people.

The therapists Sarah Moon and Steven Sandage (2019) consider this situation in counseling, and, while they do not outright reject cultural humility because of this dynamic, they endorse a nuanced approach when considering cultural humility for and as therapists of color. They acknowledge that "asking therapists of color to maintain an interpersonal stance that is other-oriented, attuned, respectful, and lacks superiority—someone already socialized into a one-down position—might lead to even further subjugation of the self" (p. 80).

Members of minoritized communities, and people who are typically on the powerless end especially of unhealthy power differentials, may already be overly used to decentering ourselves. We* may have gotten used to this as a strategy in an effort to fit in, get along, and survive, thus sacrificing accuracy in our self-assessment of our own

---

*Even though the three authors include a white man as well as two women of color, we choose to use we when talking about the experiences of BIPOC, and they when talking about white people. Part of our reasoning is to avoid reinforcing the idea that the white experience is the norm.

lived experiences, our perspectives, the value of our achievements and the beauty of who we are.

But in asking us (BIPOC) to be aware of context, cultural humility asks us to be aware of these contexts that affect us too. In asking us to redress problems of power imbalances that we have the power to redress, it is not asking us to strengthen problematic power imbalances that impact us as people of color. Cultural humility asks us to make a good faith effort to see, hear, and understand the good faith people around us. It does not ask us to tolerate intolerance.

The nuanced approach to cultural humility depends on the context, the situation, and the actors. We the authors do not have any specific guidance to offer, other than the practice of cultural humility itself: self-reflection, multiple perspectives, and a lack of defensiveness. These can guide you in determining when your practice of cultural humility might need to be strengthened by, or supplemented with, other approaches to specific individuals and contexts.

White Identity

Sarah, David, and I were watching a DEI-related webinar together when the facilitator asked participants to reflect on meaningful aspects of their identity. There was an illustration that called out likely choices: religion, race, gender, sexual orientation, profession, and so on. I thought about the things I found most meaningful, including being Native and a woman. David, a straight white guy, was at a bit of a loss—what to write down from the list provided. I said, "Well, the fact that you are white is pretty important," confused by his hesitation because I knew he was well aware of this. He replied, "But it isn't meaningful to me in that way . . . I'm not a white supremacist." Oh. If a person says, "I value my whiteness and my straightness and my maleness"—what kind of person do you think of? Probably one of those men marching in Charlottesville, Virginia, at the 2017 Unite the Right rally, chanting "We will not be replaced" and much worse. —*Lori*

But what about white people? For many white people, whiteness isn't a part of their identity that they think much about. And that is very much related to why white people are less likely to notice the impact of structural problems that disproportionately affect minoritized people. Similarly, white people are less likely to have had to accept that there are valid norms and values different from their own. When white people have to confront both that their perspective is limited and that the structures that they accept as normal are inherently unfair in their favor, it can lead to defensiveness and guilt about not having suffered the oppression that others in our society suffer.

While these realizations are important, those reactions are not helpful. Cultural humility does not let you skip out on an acknowledgement of privilege, but it also doesn't ask you to castigate yourself over it. It asks you to see the less privileged as peers and partners in seeking redress and change. It doesn't ask us to devalue ourselves, only to decenter ourselves.

AN INDIGENOUS PERSPECTIVE ON CULTURAL HUMILITY

As we the authors have been learning about and working to understand the concept of cultural humility, we started to notice an interesting pattern: Native people seem to be drawn to and accepting of the idea of cultural humility. Lori and Sarah are Native and reflected on the reasons this approach was appealing to us. We also had conversations with Native colleagues and friends who were positive about the idea, one even saying after hearing the tenets of cultural humility, "Isn't that common sense?" Of course, this is not a suggestion that all Indigenous people think alike! The intent is to highlight some broad aspects of Indigenous cultures that seem to be reflected within cultural humility practice and the idea of humility broadly.

Many definitions of cultural humility note the continuous and lifelong learning involved in this practice, recognizing the long-term effort. This seems to connect with Indigenous peoples' sense of time, which encompasses far back in time (to creation) and forward to the future, all of which affect the ways people live and act today. The Seventh Generation value from the Haudenosaunee people articulates this as thinking about the generations not yet born who will inherit a world shaped by the decisions made by those of us living today (Haudenosaunee Confederacy, n.d.). The long-term considerations of decisions for Indigenous people also seems to be a recognition of the long-term work needed to improve the world, without expectation of major change happening quickly. Therefore, engaging with others and learning and building from each interaction, as in cultural humility practice, seems to fit within existing Indigenous worldviews.

Humility itself is a concept that may parallel Indigenous people's values and teachings. For example, Tangney's framing of humility as recognizing oneself as part of a larger universe (Tangney, 2000, p. 74) aligns with the Indigenous concept of living in a connected world. Native people recognize the importance of coming together as a group both in traditional stories where collaboration meant survival and today, where everyone has to do their part to keep traditional knowledge alive. Indigenous people are here today because the ancestors worked to sustain ceremonies, practices, and family structures. Traditional stories explain the reasons why things are the way they are. Ceremonies are based on the idea of a larger universe and the collective effort needed to keep seasons, cycles, and life itself going. For many Native people, an individual is part of something bigger than oneself; individual success is often recognized as a collective success, the result of the support of family and community. This can be counter to the American/Western focus on individualism, where success is often framed as the result of one's own skill and dedication, minimizing the larger societal factors that may have led to the outcome. These Indigenous guiding concepts seem to be related to the characteristics of humility.

People who exhibit humility will recognize they are part of something bigger than themselves but also recognize their limitations and gaps in knowledge. Indigenous knowledge sharing is founded on the same concept, where gaps in knowledge are part of one's existence and knowledge acquisition is based on various factors, which may include one's age, role in the community, gender, and clan membership. Indigenous teaching structures recognize that an individual may not be able to handle specific knowledge until the appropriate time. Acknowledging that one doesn't know something is not seen as a shortcoming; one cannot know everything and should not expect to. Relatedly, when a Native community member is recognized as knowledgeable, based on the authors' experiences, often the person will be reluctant to identify as such, recognizing instead the person who taught them as the "expert," thus exhibiting humble traits.

We the authors are not the only people to have recognized the connections between cultural humility and Indigenous worldviews. Sonia Tascón and Kathomi Gatwiri (2020) identify aspects of various Indigenous cultures that they argue are centered within a cultural humility approach. These facets include deep listening when someone is speaking and the respect demonstrated when the speaker is not interrupted; recognizing people make mistakes but can learn from them; and the way practitioners and clients can be humanized and brought together through the cultural humility process (p. 13). Additionally, Loriene Roy and Leisa Moorhouse (forthcoming) have collected Indigenous adages from around the world that they use to illuminate and illustrate aspects of cultural humility.

Again, this reflection on parallels between Indigenous worldviews and the tenets of cultural humility is not meant to imply all Indigenous people exhibit or subscribe to these tenets. These reflections are included to provide another angle from which to consider the relevance and utility of cultural humility to Black, Indigenous, and people of color.

12
CONCLUSION

Cultural humility is an approach to making change while reducing harm. Cultural humility isn't about subscribing to one particular doctrine, it's about creating and maintaining relationships in the face of cultural differences as we each do our work in the world and pursue positive change. It is about approaching interactions with appreciative celebration of the other person and what they bring to the situation; deep listening; a commitment to redressing power imbalances; and treating people as peers in this effort, despite differences in status, rank, or power.

Committing to redress the negative effects of power imbalances is difficult work. Particularly if you started from a place where you were oblivious to those negative effects, those who are impacted by them may doubt your commitment. They may not appreciate or agree with your efforts. They may not see you as doing enough. They may act and speak in ways you perceive as unfair or inaccurate. Even so, cultural humility asks that you continue to listen and work toward justice and equity, apologize in a sincere and appropriate manner when you make mistakes, make amends to the wronged party, and commit to not making the same mistakes again.

We also recognize that strong emotions, including anger, are often appropriate reactions to unjust situations. We all should try to respond to emotions with grace and compassion and without defensiveness. However, we also recognize that strong emotional reactions from us can do harm to those who experience them, especially if we are in a relative position of power. But regardless of how people express their emotions and thoughts, cultural humility asks us to listen and hear, even when they are expressed in what we perceive not to be a kind or fair way.

We all must acknowledge pain and anger and do substantive work to redress wrongs, current and past, using the tools available to us. If we as individuals don't have the power to make things right ourselves, we use what power and privilege we have to speak truth to those with more power. If those people in power choose not to join us in this effort and continue instead to defend the status quo and themselves, we move on to find other partners, leaving the door open for them to learn and grow.

Cultural humility starts from a few simple principles intended to help us maintain relationships while making change. Simple is not easy, but a core set of relatively straightforward principles lowers the barrier for people to get involved and allows us to prioritize our efforts. Cultural humility also gives everyone involved options for when they inevitably get things wrong and creates an expectation that getting things wrong—and learning from it—is part of the process. And cultural humility focuses on the process, rather than outcomes or goals. It's not that goals aren't important, but the process is likely to be a long one, the goals will likely shift over time, and how we get there is at least as important as where we are going. We're all in this together, and we might as well remain (and make) friends as we go along.

And, on a final note, though we have focused much of our attention on the important work of redressing inequities, cultural humility is also about experiencing the joy and beauty of living with and in and as a part of the dazzling diversity of humanity.

We wish you all the joy in the world.

ACRL Racial and Ethnic Diversity Committee. (2012). Diversity standards: Cultural competency for academic librarians: Approved by the ACRL Board of Directors, April 2012. *College & Research Libraries News, 73*(9), 551–561. https://doi.org/10.5860/crln.73.9.8835

Aguilar, Paulita, Sarah R. Kostelecky, Lori Townsend, and Margie Montanez. (2022). *Missing and Murdered Indigenous Women and Girls (MMIWG)*. University of New Mexico, University Libraries. https://libguides.unm.edu/mmiw.

American Library Association (2009). *ALA's Core Competences of Librarianship*. https://www.ala.org/educationcareers/sites/ala.org.educationcareers/files/content/careers/corecomp/corecompetences/finalcorecompstat09.pdf

Alabi, J. (2015). Racial microaggressions in academic libraries: Results of a survey of minority and non-minority librarians. *Journal of Academic Librarianship, 41*(1), 47–53. https://doi.org/10.1016/j.acalib.2014.10.008

Buri, J. R. (1988). The nature of humankind, authoritarianism, and self-esteem. *Journal of Psychology and Christianity, 7*(1), 32–38.

Crenshaw, K. (1989). Demarginalizing the intersection of race and sex: Black feminist critique of antidiscrimination doctrine, feminist theory and antiracist politics. *University of Chicago Legal Forum, 1989*, 139–168.

Cross, T. L., Bazron, B., Dennis, K., & Issacs, M. (1989). *Towards a culturally competent system of care: A monograph on effective services for minority children who are severely emotionally disturbed*. Georgetown University Child Development Center. https://eric.ed.gov/?id=ED330171

Deitering, A.-M. (2015, April 10). *Culture is what people do*. Info-Fetishist. https://info-fetishist.org/2015/04/10/culture-is-what-people-do/

Delgado, R., & Stefancic, J. (2001). *Critical race theory: An introduction*. New York University Press.

Giulietti, C., Tonin, M., & Vlassopoulos, M. (2019). Racial discrimination in local public services: A field experiment in the United States. *Journal of the European Economic Association, 17*(1), 165–204. https://doi.org/10.1093/jeea/jvx045

Gourlay, L. (2009) Threshold practices: becoming a student through academic literacies. *London Review of Education, 7*(2):181–192. https://doi.org/10.1080/14748460903003626

Haudenosaunee Confederacy. (n.d.) *Values*. https://www.haudenosauneeconfederacy.com/values/

Hurley, D. A., Kostelecky, S. R., & Townsend, L. (2019). Cultural humility in libraries. *Reference Services Review*, 47(4), 544–555. https://doi.org/10.1108/RSR-06-2019-0042

Kostelecky, Sarah. (2022). *The Dakota Access Pipeline: Native American Perspectives*. University of New Mexico, University Libraries. https://libguides.unm.edu/DAPL.

Linfield, S. L. (1960). Looking around. *Harvard Business Review*, 38(5), 41–42, 44, 46, 50, 166, 168, 170, 172.

Meyer, J. H. F., & Land, R. (2005). Threshold concepts and troublesome knowledge (2): Epistemological considerations and a conceptual framework for teaching and learning. *Higher Education*, 49(3), 373–388. https://doi.org/10.1007/s10734-004-6779-5

Mitch Landrieu's speech on the removal of Confederate monuments in New Orleans. (2017, December 22). *The New York Times*.

Moon, S. H., & Sandage, S. J. (2019). Cultural Humility for People of Color: Critique of Current Theory and Practice. *Journal of Psychology and Theology*, 47(2), 76–86. https://doi.org/10.1177/0091647119842407

Moore, D. A., & Schatz, D. (2017). The three faces of overconfidence. *Social and Personality Psychology Compass*, 11(8), e12331. https://doi.org/10.1111/spc3.12331

Mungin, M. (Forthcoming). Reflections on culturally humble practice in bibliography, scholarship, and readers' advisory: A case study. In S. R. Kostelecky, L. Townsend, & D. A. Hurley (Eds.), *Hopeful visions, practical actions: Cultural humility in library work*. ALA Editions.

Office of the Press Secretary (2016, September 23). *Remarks by the President at Reception in Honor of the National Museum of African American History and Culture*. White House. https://obamawhitehouse.archives.gov/the-press-office/2016/09/23/remarks-president-reception-honor-national-museum-african-american

Overall, P. M. (2009). Cultural competence: A conceptual framework for library and information science professionals. *The Library Quarterly*, 79(2), 175–204. https://doi.org/10.1086/597080

Oxford University Press. (2019a). Microaggression. In *OED Online*. https://www.oed.com/view/Entry/64098026

Oxford University Press. (2019b). Pride. In *OED Online*. https://www.oed.com/view/Entry/151185

Peterson, C., & Seligman, M. E. P. (2004). *Character strengths and virtues: A handbook and classification*. American Psychological Association.

Priceman, M. (1965). Inter-cultural competence and the American businessman. *Training Directors Journal*, 19(3), 4–10.

Roy, L. & Moorhouse, L. (Forthcoming). "Time is a ship that never casts anchor": Indigenous adages in promoting cultural humility. In S. R. Kostelecky, L. Townsend, & D. A. Hurley (Eds.), *Hopeful visions, practical actions: Cultural humility in library work.* ALA Editions.

Sorrell, R. (Forthcoming). Embedding Diné culture in individual and institutional cultural humility practices: A view from the tribal college library. In S. Kostelecky, L. Townsend, & D. A. Hurley (Eds.), *Hopeful visions, practical actions: Cultural humility in library work.* ALA Editions.

Stone slave auction block from Hagerstown, Maryland. (n.d.). National Museum of African American History and Culture. https://nmaahc.si.edu/object/nmaahc_2015.213

Tangney, J. P. (2000). Humility: Theoretical perspectives, empirical findings and directions for future research. *Journal of Social and Clinical Psychology, 19*(1), 70–82.

Tascón, S., & Gatwiri, K. (2020). Towards cultural humility: Theorising cultural competence as institutionalised whiteness. *Social Work & Policy Studies: Social Justice, Practice and Theory, 3*(1), Article 1. https://openjournals.library.sydney.edu.au/index .php/SWPS/article/view/14406

Templeton, J. M. (1997). *Worldwide laws of life: 200 eternal spiritual principles.* Templeton Foundation Press.

Tervalon, M., & Murray-García, J. (1998). Cultural humility versus cultural competence: A critical distinction in defining physician training outcomes in multicultural education. *Journal of Health Care for the Poor and Underserved, 9*(2), 117–125. https://doi.org/10.1353/hpu.2010.0233

Tharp, B. M. (2005). *Defining 'culture' and 'organizational culture': From anthropology to the office [White Paper].* Haworth. https://web.archive.org/web/20101227124915/ https://www.haworth.com/en-us/Knowledge/Workplace-Library/Documents/ Defining-Culture-and-Organizationa-Culture_5.pdf

University of New Mexico. (n.d.). *Official enrollment reports: Office of Institutional Analytics.* http://oia.unm.edu/facts-and-figures/official-enrollment-reports.html

US Bureau of Labor Statistics. (2021). Household data annual averages: Employed persons by detailed occupation, sex, race, and Hispanic or Latino Ethnicity. *Labor Force Statistics from the Current Population Survey.* Accessed March 30, 2021. https:// www.bls.gov/cps/cpsaat11.pdf

ABOUT THE AUTHORS

DAVID HURLEY is the discovery and web librarian for the University of New Mexico University Libraries. In addition to cultural humility, he writes and presents on search, reference services, and information literacy. He was previously the director of the Diné College Libraries on the Navajo Nation, chief of the library development bureau at the New Mexico State Library, and branch and digital services manager for the Public Library of Albuquerque and Bernalillo County. With Sarah Kostelecky and Paulita Aguilar, David coedited "Sharing Knowledge and Smashing Stereotypes: Representing Native American, First Nation, and Indigenous Realities in Library Collections," a special double issue of the journal *Collection Management*.

LORI TOWNSEND (Shoshone-Paiute) is the learning services coordinator and a social sciences librarian for the University of New Mexico Libraries. Her research interests include threshold concepts and information literacy, cultural humility, source evaluation, and genre theory. Lori holds a BA in history from the University of New Mexico and an MLIS from San José State University. Before coming to UNM, she worked as the electronic collections librarian at California State University, East Bay, from 2005 to 2010. She is coauthor, along with Amy R. Hofer and Silvia Lin Hanick, of the book *Transforming Information Literacy Instruction: Threshold Concepts in Theory and Practice* (Libraries Unlimited, 2018); she and Silvia Lin Hanick are series editors for the just-launched Libraries Unlimited series on Teaching Information Literacy Today.

SARAH R. KOSTELECKY (Zuni Pueblo) is the director of Digital Initiatives and Scholarly Communication (DISC) for University of New Mexico Libraries. Her research focuses on outreach efforts to underrepresented communities, diversity in academic libraries and library collections, and Native American language resources. Previously at UNM, Sarah has served as the education librarian and access services librarian in the Indigenous Nations Library Program (INLP). She earned both her MA in information resources and library science and her BA in sociology from the University of Arizona. Prior to working at UNM Libraries, Sarah was the library director at the Institute of American Indian Arts (IAIA) in Santa Fe, New Mexico, the premiere educational institution for contemporary Native American arts and cultures. Along with David Hurley and Paulita Aguilar, she coedited "Sharing Knowledge and Smashing Stereotypes: Representing Native American, First Nation, and Indigenous Realities in Library Collections," a special double issue of the journal *Collection Management*. Sarah has enjoyed working in a variety of libraries including university, public, tribal college, and museum.

INDEX